"If you want to change the world, pick up a pen and write."

—Martin Luther, *Theologian*

POETRY on our terms

Winners of the 2014 7GP 7th Grade Poetry Contest

Aaron Williams, Editor

Sponsored and published by

ISBN: 978-0-616-00088-5

Printed in the United States of America

Book layout and design by Alexis Turim

Aaron Williams, Editor

Cynthia R. Buehler, Assistant Editor

CONTENTS

FOREWORD

Dear Readers,

After 43 years of literacy-related classroom teaching, I was attracted to The 7th Grade Poetry Foundation (7GP) by its mission to produce authentic student writing. Last year's anthology convinced me that 7GP was special. The poetry was creative, unique and meaningful. Students' writings reflected joys, achievements, memories, challenges and pain.

This year, as 7GP's first Educator Liaison, I witnessed how students' work improved with enhanced teacher support and individualized feedback. Also, the chance for young writers to present their work beyond a classroom setting seemed to influence student involvement. With bravery and confidence, the poets have connected with larger audiences in print and in person. As a result, the pride of student achievement is shared when the best efforts of students, educators, families, and community partners converge. I know of no other research-based, nationwide initiative like 7GP that builds community across cultures through the words of 7th graders.

Some think 7th graders can't understand or write about certain topics or subjects. Actually, young writers are astute at discerning situations and in making the world come alive through their words.

This anthology provides a rich reading experience and is a treasure to be celebrated and shared.

With respect and gratitude to the young authors,

Cynthia R. Buehler, M.Ed., M.A.
Educator Liaison, 7th Grade Poetry Foundation

PREFACE

Poetry on Our Terms: Winners of the 2014 7GP 7th Grade Poetry Contest is the result of the nation's most inclusive 7th grade poetry writing program. More than 1,250 schools of every type, including charter, faith-based, public and private, were invited to be a part of the program.

From 120 participating schools, 8,100 students were given the freedom of creative self-expression through poetry: to write their own poem about any theme and in any style. Each school selected one winner based solely on the words written by the student. Educators balanced local, state, and federal guidelines for curriculum and testing, a disruptive series of snow days and impeding personal and professional circumstances. Despite these challenges, they inspired students to write more than 4,200 poems specifically for this competition. This book celebrates the 120 poets and their poems that were chosen by their respective schools.

A copy of this anthology was given to each winning poet, their school, and community library. The book is used to motivate next year's students. Several poems will be incorporated into the next 7GP lesson plan.

With expanded outreach, we strive to change America's perception of poetry. In past years, 7th grade students and their educators struggled to believe that poets in this age group wrote poems of such high quality and diverse content. Now everyone will have a chance to read and appreciate the welcome creativity, wisdom and emotions that 7th grade students can share with their peers and their communities.

INTRODUCTION

This book is full of surprises. The tears and triumphs of 7th graders—their loves and disappointments, habits and quirks—are embedded into every page. After decades of reading poetry anthologies by all levels of poets, I have become convinced that some of the most skilled and honest poetry comes from the young people who write for this contest. From poem to poem, stanza to stanza, you can see how the contest's freedom empowers each generation of newly published poets to celebrate their voices.

This book is about freedom and trust. Inside, you will find sonnets, haikus, and rhyming odes. While one writer bemoans the horrors of war, another proudly salutes the military victories of our country. Native American students write about themes influenced by their culture. Elsewhere, there is the pain of being orphaned, the appreciation of family and belonging, and several close examinations of bullying. We trusted students to use their freedom wisely and we are proud of their achievement.

This book is about respect—respect for young authors and their ability to tell us something important. Poetry is better on their terms, where the craft of writing and love of language exhibited by each poet clearly speaks for itself. Each page offers a separate journey into the mind of a 7th grader and leaves you feeling amazement and wonder at the literary prowess of this age group. Cherish it. This is an exciting read.

Aaron Williams
Editor

The 7th Grade Poetry Foundation™

ABOUT 7GP

The 7th Grade Poetry Foundation is a 501(c)(3) charitable organization based in St. Louis, Missouri. Its vision is to create a national rite of passage for every 7th grade student in every school in every community to compete in school-based poetry writing contests. Its mission is to transform young lives and improve classrooms by creating a writing revolution that gives all students the chance to have their poetic voices celebrated.

Through filmed poetry reading events, the foundation showcases winning 7th grade poetry that unites students, families, schools, communities and, ultimately, an entire country. It provides its services and programming at no cost to schools and their participants through creative collaborations with generous community resources and partners.

In our fourth year of operation, the organization has seen tremendous growth: starting with only schools within the City of St. Louis, to now including schools from Alaska to Florida and from Arizona to Massachusetts. We have learned that geographic expansion produces a greater diversity in students' poetry themes and styles. We also gained more insight how our program impacts students and classrooms.

Beginning in the Fall of 2013, the foundation donated its innovative *7GP 7th Grade Poetry Lesson Plan* to all registered educators. The plan incorporated past 7GP winning poems into daily lessons that helped educators achieve their curriculum goals and showed new groups of students the potential they had for writing poetry.

For more information, please visit www.7GP.org.

WHY 7TH GRADE?

Reading and writing poetry has become part of the standardized curriculum for 7th grade classrooms in nearly every state in the country. This is partially due to the Common Core State Standards Initiative, a nationwide program developed by teachers, school administrators and experts to provide a clear and consistent framework to prepare children for college and the workforce. Since poetry related activities already occur in 7th grade classrooms, The 7th Grade Poetry Foundation designed its approach to enhance school-based outcomes. We believe that 7th grade is the ideal school year to create an educational literary arts rite of passage for student self-expression between their first and last days of school.

Published reports from the RAND Corporation, the National Commission on Writing, and the Alliance for Excellent Education indicate that our program supports their recommendations how to cultivate demand for the literary arts, to create a writing revolution, and make writing instruction a high priority by engaging students in writing opportunities. In order to develop a positive lifetime relationship with writing, they advise educators to find new ways to help students realize that writing is fun, should be shared, and can provide a sense of ownership and pride.

2014 7GP Winning Poems

Padraic Riordan
ST. MARGARET OF SCOTLAND SCHOOL

Parallel Universe

A simple flip of the page; a calm, musty odor
Sucks me out of this world, and puts me where it pleases.
I am at the mercy of the word; I'm at the whim of the sentence.
I see each place as an outsider; I cannot intervene, or change how it ends,
There is sorrow, joy, greed, despair, and hope, yet I love every moment of it.
At times I cry with the characters, I'm shocked at the evil in the villain's heart.
I'm there to witness every conflict; and I know all secrets, even when
the character doesn't.
I see into the minds of strange people; people who aren't even real,
And feel for every action, which simply reflects the author's personality,
I see historic events in far-off lands, which I know I'll never visit
But feel as if I'm there, even at this very moment.
I envy every author, with the power to catch one's heart in such a way,
And so when I pick up a book off the shelf and open the front cover
I'm exhilarated, excited, and prepared
To enter a parallel universe.

Kaleb Palmer
NATIVE AMERICAN COMMUNITY ACADEMY

The Blood Raven

The Raven made from Ash and Blood.
The ashes of our reservations and hesitations.
The blood of our rez and the blood of our ancestors.

Some children chant, "The Blood Raven!
Come save us from the rotting of our world!"
Once he would come and save these poor children
from Sorrow and Time with Verse and Rhyme
with Iambic Pentameter and with Pantoums and Haikus.

The great Edgar Allen Poe wrote with such grace,
"Quoth the raven nevermore."
If only there was pain nevermore, insane nevermore,
death nevermore, blood nevermore.

The Blood Raven is our protector.
Though his eyes are pure red and his body as black as obsidian,
the children no longer quote him.
Even in their darkest times they do not chant to him because
the Vulture of Ignorance
has plucked the children's eyes out
so that they can no longer read
the Chant of the
Blood Raven.

The Raven made from Ash and Blood.
The ashes of our reservations and hesitations.
The blood of our rez and the blood of our ancestors.

Jordan Mattsen
NEW PALTZ MIDDLE SCHOOL

Sand

I am torn between two elements
Two worlds question my judgment of the other,
Constantly colliding,

The seagulls of the ocean screech
And the bees of grass buzz in my ears

Each conniving against each other

I am the being of two worlds,
I am thrown from wall to wall,
Each brick a flimsy certain thought,
Forced to imprint my mind

"Blue eyes," says the sea,
I see only green,
"Green irises," confirms the land

The land is my homeland
As the ocean is too vast,

So, like the land,
I should have these green spying things,
I should have a strong hold of my roots,
I should be wise.

The ocean spray calms me,
As the grass itches my skin

So, like water,
I should be free yet smooth,
I should know my place amongst rivers,

I should have a path.

I realize, now
I am a single element,
I have been collided,
These sounds in my head are my own creation,
There is no conniving,
My eyes are teal
And I have no homeland

Why am I not on my clear path?

I am Sand
The creation of Earth and Water
And I know my coursing path between both.

Micalan Hampton
MOST HOLY TRINITY CATHOLIC SCHOOL AND ACADEMY

As I Look Around

As I look around
I see black, white and mix
I wonder if I am known
Or just another little girl from St. Louis

As I look around
I see the poor and the rich
I wonder why such a divide
And, how did the world get like this

As I look around
I see the lights flashing in my face
I wonder what the hurry is
Even though there's not a race

As I look around
I see how being famous can be
I wonder if it is worth the drama
Or is it better to just be me

I'm getting older and defining who I am
And I am saying
I AM HERE

Marie Divecchio
HAWTHORNE VALLEY WALDORF SCHOOL

An Ode to the Jumping Horse

The feeling of power as it surges
The momentary suspense
As horse to its rider merges
And time seems to stop, condense

The impact as hooves meet ground
The check of balance and weight
And again the world has sound
This is destined to be their fate

The smell of fragrant green pines
The dark brown of their trunks
As polished leather shines
And ahead a row of jumps

The final exertion of strength
The last bend in the course
As they gallop along the last length
An ode to the jumping horse.

PJ Wuennenberg
MOST SACRED HEART CATHOLIC SCHOOL

A Storm

It was a calm yet very dark night
The full moon was shining very bright.

I was in the back of a car on an old country road.
I was lying on a blanket my own aunt sewed.

I was awoken from a very long slumber
By the strange sound of a rumble of thunder.

I looked out the window through the fog's thick shroud
And saw lightning, thunder, and a cumulonimbus cloud.

The large thunderhead towered over the sky.
I soon became very frightened. Oh my! Oh my!

The rain began to pound on our thick windshield,
But no water came through. It was very sealed.

When I got to my house not a soul could be found.
Neither my father nor sister was walking around.

I then heard a very peculiar sound.
It was a tornado siren! I raced all around.

I ran through the hallways and right down the stairs
To find that my sister was already down there.

We waited in the basement and heard the whole house rumble.
We heard the tornado grunt and grumble.

After the storm, our house had not met its demise,
But it makes me wonder what would happen if another storm should arise?

MacKenzie Hunter
SHARON CENTER SCHOOL

After All

What is growing up
Growing up is when memories are made
The kind you don't forget
When you realize you're not too old for Disney movies
But you greet them as old friends
When you find who your true friends are
The ones who will always be by your side
When society holds you back
And you break free
When homework piles up
And you struggle
When you like someone
And they break your heart
When quotes are your life
And your camera roll is full of them
When you are told what is cool
And you do it
When you grow apart from your family
But they are still your everything
Growing up is Friday movies
That no one goes to anymore
When you try to fit in
And still you are different
When life gets hard
But no matter what, you don't give up
All the rough patches in life are just pieces to a greater story
Take the drama
Play the part that you've always wanted to be
Life is just a giant riddle that people are overthinking
No wonder no one's found the answer
But it's so simple
Grow up at your own pace
After all
It is your life

Zach Mueller
ST. STEPHEN PROTOMARTYR SCHOOL

A Day in The Boy Scouts of America

Waking up at 6:00 A.M. or before
Sometimes sleeping on the forest floor
No matter at which camp you stay
That's a day in the B.S.A

Cooking food with your friends
Sitting through a merit badge class that never ends
Tying knots and learning the Boy Scout way
That's a day in the B.S.A.

Carving a stick into a wooden spear
Trying to sleep without any fear
Hopefully you enjoy your stay
That's a day in the B.S.A.

Going places you've never gone before
Knowing the next day will never be a bore
No scout will be turned away
That's a day in the B.S.A.

Staying up late to see the stars
Loading the stuff back into the cars
Hopefully you enjoyed your stay
See you next year at the B.S.A.

Michael Milk
NORTH MIDDLE SCHOOL

Drum Heartbeats

The native drum is a symbol,
not only a symbol but a heart.

When I hear the drum…
the singing…
I feel my heart beating with the drum,
and I wonder…

am I the follower or the leader?

Then my heart beats faster,
faster,
and faster
Then stops.
Just like that.

I go blank

a man was sitting there and he said to me
"Break the bad rules…make good ones,"

and then I awoke like a Dracula coming out of his longest slumber.

I said,

"I'm the leader."

Paris Dukes
LANGSTON MIDDLE SCHOOL

How Freedom Came to Be

There was a man named Martin, last name King,
He had a very inspirational dream.
His dream was to free the Blacks,
He wanted them to stop getting whacked.
The time of slavery flew by,
Like a little birdie in the sky.
The people screamed, "God forgive us,
We no longer want to ride in the back of the bus."

They were tired of the Whites and going to jail,
They didn't have any money for bail.
Martin's dream was for Whites to come clean,
Think positive thoughts and not be so mean.
Instead of Whites getting lost in their own minds,
The way they treated Blacks had no reason or rhyme.
Petrified and defeated, they prepared their righteous minds,
They had to get ready for better spiritual times.

Martin preached, "I have a dream today,"
He announced his words, what he had to say.
As he spoke the people cried and cried,
They tried not to show it, inside they had died.
Martin's words grew on them like a tree.
They knew one day they would be totally free.
Martin was always by their side,
And their hearts were filled with love and pride.

In the end, they finally won their respect and a place,
Proud, strong, and defiant the Black race.

Bradley Estrada
ST. RICHARD SCHOOL

WAR

War. What's the need for it
As we spill the blood of our brothers and sisters across this earth?
All of us just waiting for a rebirth.
Fighting over land and fossil fuel.
Yeah, some people think it's cool.
But only if they knew of what really happens.
Families getting their children taken forever.
Babies that will never get to see their father or mother.
While we sit comfortably here at home under this country's freedom.
The freedom bought by soldiers, every single one.
But everything has a price, including our freedom.
And for that we can thank the men and women on the frontline.
Just waiting, ready to die for us.
War. Ashes to Ashes, Dust to Dust.

Hypatia Her
OAKDALE MIDDLE SCHOOL

Fear

Some kids in this world live in fear everyday
They're scared of what might happen so they'll just say
"I think I might die today"
They can't even speak their own mind
They can't express their own emotions
They meet somebody that's not very kind
And puts them in a place which causes a lot of commotion
They hold on to life—they truly tried
But by morning they found out another one died
Their thoughts roam, "Will this ever be justified?"
Fear is their life
Laughter is a mystery
Until one day *their* life will be history…

Dedicated to the kids who have experienced or are currently experiencing war.

Aaron Williams
CLARKSBURG ELEMENTARY SCHOOL

War

Men sobbing
from the loss of a friend

Women crying
from the loss of their children

Who creates the pain
of war:
the creator or the creation?

Is war a crime
or
an endeavor?

Only the man who creates it
knows its truth.

Nicolas Joy
NAMASTE CHARTER SCHOOL

The Meadow

As I look beyond
I see a meadow
a canvas of God's paint
the purple violets burst in joy when it rains
the blue grass so beautiful in its gaze
but it is simply a painting
a disguise
for something dark and corrupt

The grass is hellish green
and the violets turn into roses in the black rain
roses filled with red blood of 800 soldiers
God's paint
turned into the devil's spit
the devil's spit is eternal
in the meadow.

Ashley Rice
CARR LANE MIDDLE SCHOOL

Day Dreams

In the flowery fields of life, the plains
of hope in which people who
dream float on the clouds
of faith because sometimes
between the orange and
the indigo is the emerald
sunset improbable
green holding day
and night
apart.

Danny Behlmann
ALL SAINTS CATHOLIC SCHOOL

Vigilance

It is always there.
It has served us, our community,
    and especially our country.
It has always been there.

From the icy waters of Valley Forge,
    to the bloody swamps of Vietnam.
From the ruined fields of Shiloh, Tennessee,
    to the dry deserts of Pakistan.
It was there in both World Wars
    and it is even on the moon.

Our flag,
a symbol of freedom,
stood strong through hardships of the Depression and 9/11.
It also stood proudly in the fall of the Berlin Wall
and when Blacks, Whites, and women all became equal.

Our flag, with…
…Red stripes, representing the valor
and bloodshed of American men and women
lost in war for this country.
…White, representing the purity of American spirit and heart.
…Blue, representing the vigilance from sea to shining sea
of the great country of America.
…thirteen stripes for the thirteen original colonies.
…fifty stars for the fifty states.
Uniting all of us as patriots.

Our flag was there.
It is there.
It will be there.
Forever vigilant.

God bless America.

Tyvon Herman
LITTLEBURG ELEMENTARY SCHOOL

Lakota People

Lakota
Proud, Happy
HELPING, WILLING, GIVING
Generosity, Courage, Respect, Wisdom
GIVING, LEARNING, SHARING
Great-Hearted, Noble
Sicangu

Sangam Rai
NEW AMERICAN PREPARATORY ACADEMY

My Country, Nepal

My country is small,
But it is beautiful.

My country is old,
But old is gold.

I don't only respect
My country of Nepal,

I respect the whole World.
I love my culture because we celebrate together!

In 2012 I came to the United States,
But still celebrate my culture with its beautiful red flag.

I love my country
Not just for the mountains,

Rivers, and forests, but because
Nepal is my Motherland!

Shelby Little Shield
SPRING CREEK ELEMENTARY SCHOOL

Where I'm From

From glasses and shortness and tall
From songs my mother sang
From running horses across the plains
From from family laughs and cries
From hellos and goodbyes
From Indian blood that is true
From creative minds that make me creative too
From kindness and laughter
From a community that is loud
From smart minds
From sunrise to sunset
I am from South Dakota
My home is where my family lives.

Faith Kassebaum
FIRST BAPTIST CHRISTIAN ACADEMY

Gone Forever

The clock ticks faster.
Days became hours.
In only minutes,
He's leaving today.

He's like my brother,
So bright and happy.
Sweet, young visitor,
He's leaving today.

My heart beats fiercely,
Louder and faster.
It never ceases,
He's leaving today.

My head keeps spinning,
I can't stay focused.
My ears are ringing.
He's leaving today.

What else can I do?
I'm watching him leave.
He's gone forever.
Not one final word.

One month has vanished.
Dima had to leave.
Back home to Russia,
He's not ours to keep.

He left with no tears.
No sorrow. No doubt.
Not a word of thanks.
He's gone forever!

Anthony Lachenicht
GATEWAY SCIENCE ACADEMY OF ST. LOUIS

Life

Life always has surprises in store
Sometimes too good to ignore
You never know what will come next
Always finding out might not be best

Life has its twists and turns
What life is all about you will learn
Life has its ups and downs
It will sometimes make you frown

Life is stressful
Life is mysterious
Life is good

Theresa Solari
IMMACULATE HEART OF MARY CATHOLIC SCHOOL

Footprints

Footprints in snow
Trailing behind me
Marking my path
More snow falls
I look back
My imprints disappear
I'm all alone
In snowy wonderland
I keep going
On and on
Leaving behind my
Footprints in snow

Josh Heuvel-Horwitz
RONDOUT VALLEY MIDDLE SCHOOL

Rainbows

Rainbows
Where the wind blows
No one knows where the rainbow goes
Chase, chase, chase as you like
You'll never touch rainbows, try as you might
The rainbows sight avoids even flight
So it's not quite worth the fight
Artificial rainbows, a temporary fix
Although it's the same as looking at sticks
Or bricks or hearing click, click, clicks
Where none dare go
Rainbow

Jack Nikolai
ST. AMBROSE CATHOLIC SCHOOL

Life and Death

Life is an explosion of color into a barren world.
Colors turn into many beings that make up the life of our planet.
Some colors have smells like the sweet fragrance of the pink flower.
The colors make sounds to communicate with each other.
Some colors eat other colors for nutrition.
Some colors mix together to feel another's touch.
Like lying on the soft green grass, life feels exceptionally amazing.

Death however is ruin and loss,
The feeling of never seeing oneself again.
The sound of crying and sobbing hurts the very soul.
The whole subconscious of oneself is in pain and agony.
The sadness is so strong you can smell it.

With the joys and happiness of life,
All good things though, must come to an end,
Followed with death's agony and pain.
This is why we need to live life as we can in the present,
Not worrying about the future,
Nor dwelling in the past.

Mackenzie Goff
HILLSBORO R-3 JUNIOR HIGH SCHOOL

Stranger

I never really got to know you,
But I always will love you.
When we met, you could never talk.
I never even saw you walk,
But you were always there.

When we went to your house, I would always say, "Hi."
You couldn't answer; I wanted to cry.
I've seen pictures of me and you looking so happy.
But then I was just a baby.
We were robbed by disease.

They say dementia stole you away
Even though I asked for miracles each time I prayed.
My hope is we will soon be connected.
For now my heart feels dissected.
Aching tears continue to flow.

RIP Grandpa

Shatavia Franklin
OWL CREEK SCHOOL

In the Moment

As I stand here, I feel the breeze
    Slither down my spine
        My hair flowing with the wind
            Birds chirping, bees buzz
                It's almost as if time has stopped

A single moment frozen
    A dog's mouth open ready to catch a Frisbee
        A boy's ice cream drip, drip, dripping
            But the drip hangs suspended in mid air
                Leaves hang swirling on the breeze
                    And, for a moment the breath of the world is held

What happens next?
    What happened right before?
        I don't care.
            I'm in the moment.

KyJuan Holmes
ST. LOUIS THE KING SCHOOL AT THE CATHEDRAL

Laughing

I love to smile and laugh
Laughing is fabulous and fun
Laughing is hard sometimes
Especially when you're trying to run

Whenever I laugh
I always think it's nice
It makes me think of jokes
About animals chewing rice

Laughing is real
Angry is fake
Sometimes when I get sleepy
Laughing helps me stay awake

Amaya Earls
IMMANUEL LUTHERAN DAY SCHOOL

The Memory Dress

It sits on a hanger in my closet
Looking so beautiful and delicate
All yellow with pink flowers on it
When I look at it
It makes me remember her on that very sad day
My Grandma looked so beautiful
The way she laid in the casket, it made me cry
We drove in the limo to the cemetery
It was raining
My dress started to get muddy at the bottom
While standing there watching the men bury her
Every time I look at the dress hanging in my closet
I think of that day

Dani Fischer
PARKWAY WEST MIDDLE SCHOOL

Moving Past Autumn

Autumn comes quicker each year
And so do the memories of you
Floods of them
From where I buried them last year

Raking leaves by your side
Knowing what lay in store for us when we finished
A pile of leaves
That could be anything we wanted

Our faces red with cold
As we sipped hot chocolate
And picked the leaves
Out of each other's hair

The trees we climbed
To take pictures from the top of the world
And the forts we made
Larger and grander each time

Sitting at your kitchen table
Eating noodles in silence
Reassured
By the other's presence

Now I can't stand fall
Every shade of orange
Every crunch of the leaves
Every breath of crisp air

It makes me believe that you will be back
I stare at the phone for hours
Willing you to call and invite me over
But deep down knowing it's not possible

I go to bed at night
Wishing and hoping on every star
That we can share one more evening under
The twinkling windows to heaven

And when our song comes on the radio
I try to sing along
But I can't
I don't know your part

How can I move on
When you were half my past
Half my life
Half of me

I try to forget
Like everyone tells me to
But every year
Autumn comes again

Dejure Blackman
ACADEMY OF ENV. SCIENCE AND MATHEMATICS

Grief

Grief pulls you down deep
Slides up your spine and curls
Around your feet
Wraps around your mind so that
You can no longer think
Grief takes your happiness
like a highly skilled thief
like an alligator with two rows of sharp teeth
Don't slip into the vicious jaws of stress and grief

Nailahni M. Thompson
DESERT PALMS ELEMENTARY

The Tunnel

Hope is waiting in an
Icy
Damp
Murky
Tunnel for a lifetime

Then seeing a speck of light
At the end of the tunnel
You know you will
Feel the warm sun coat your skin

Your feet ache and your stomach
grumbles

But the desire to be set free from the trap
Of the tunnel is too large

You know as long as you
Walk up to the bright light at the end of the tunnel
All of the troubles of the world
Will be diminished
And you will be set free.

Michel Quintana
ST. CECILIA SCHOOL AND ACADEMY

Crystal Tears

I look up into the clear sky.
Tears run like liquid crystals down my face.
They turn into ice.
I see red all around me.
I feel like I've been crying so much.
Why does it feel like blood is running down from my eyes?
Through the window I see my family full of disappointment.
I see hands reaching out like a tree, but I can't reach back.
My tears run down my face again.

What is that thing in the mirror?
Is that me?
In the reflection why do I look like I am dead?
My pain cuts me apart section by section.

Is this the time, or is it too late?
Should I stay or go away?
I can't take it anymore living in this world.
It's ice cold.
I want others to see I have feelings too.
Look into my eyes.
Tell me if I'm fine or not.
But you tell me.

I don't say things about my feelings.
I'm scared you will make fun of me.
The beats in my heart are going slower every day.
I reach in the dark.
I long for light.
I see my friends so happy.

Why can`t I be happy like them?
Every day I know I will rest with a cold heart.
The next thing I know I'm gone.
I`m the talk of the people now.
As I'm laid in the box all I can hear is
"Poor girl."

And I wake up in a different world.

Kurt Unger
OUR REDEEMER LUTHERAN SCHOOL

My Last Day

I lay awake on my hospital bed
Everyone around me is sad
Sitting next to me, my son and my wife
The doctor said it was the end of my life
My daughter was crying
She knew I was dying
My wife said it would be alright
She said I should go to the light
"I love you," I said with a smile,
"And I'll see my family in a while"
Then the light came to me
My family was with me
With everyone I ever knew
People gone long ago
Elvis Presley
Vincent Van Gogh
There is a throne
Huge and made of stone
And sitting there,
An ancient being
I knew what I was seeing
I walked around
My forever home
Then Elizabeth II
Offered me a scone

Emily Hirshman
CROSSROADS COLLEGE PREPARATORY SCHOOL

Baker

starts with basics
flour
water
eggs
a pinch of sugar
for sweetness
an everyday bread
nothing special

kneads dough with rough hands
rough from a life of baking
and not much more
tired
content
into the oven
finished
job done

bored in the same routine
wanting more flavor
needs a new beginning
and he waits for himself to rise

Gracie Scanga
OUR LADY QUEEN OF PEACE SCHOOL

Breakfast

This morning, I smelled outside my door,
pancakes, sausage, eggs and more.
So I ran down the stairs
and pulled one of the chairs
to enjoy delicious breakfast galore.

My mom and dad had gone away,
so my sister is watching me today.
So she and I ate
What was delicious and great.
And off to school I went away.

When I got home, I took the shoes off my feet.
Then, I got tucked in my sheet.
Then I went to bed
with dreams in my head
of tomorrow, of breakfast, which I will eat.

Brianna Parson
CARONDELET LEADERSHIP ACADEMY

Dreams

When the sun goes down, my day is not done.
I close my eyes and fall into a land of fun
Where trees talk and people fly,
And days drift slowly by.
The apples are caramel, the clouds candy,
And the number of friends is many.
But my dreams aren't always so sweet.
For the danger comes from a stranger I meet.
When my only friends are myself and I,
It is then that a stranger walks by.
He whispers in my ear nothing but a lie.
I follow him to a stream
Where he walks in and lets out a convincing scream.
I run to help but realize it's too late,
That my foolish mistake determined my fate.
The water grabs my leg and pulls me in,
Dragging me faster than the roaring wind.
I open my eyes right then
And realize it's over again.

Marlene Dominguez
COCHITI MIDDLE SCHOOL

Voices in the Night

I hear them whispering in the night,
When they're talking it doesn't feel right.
They tell me different than what I want to hear.
Why does it seem like they're near?
I wonder if they're always around.
I can't see them but I hear their sound.
When I laugh at them,
The lights go dim.
I wonder if they're only in my mind.
Why do they keep my heart in a bind?
I beg them to speak,
But all I hear is my own shriek.
When they're finally done,
It's always when it's the rise of the sun.

Alyssa Benavidez
PECOS MIDDLE SCHOOL

Wake Me Up

Wake me up when it's all over
Wake me up when I'm free
When I can wake up for school and
Wear whatever I want, look however I want
Without getting judged

Wake me up when I can
Laugh and not be uncomfortable
Wake me up when people don't
Get bullied because of their weight,
Height or looks

Wake me up when everyone is
Free from a monster inside their own head
Wake me up when
We all have a friend that
Will stick with us through everything

Wake me up when everyone
Gets along, wake me up when we
Could all feel free,
Wake me up when it's all over

Ashley Nicole Hrdina
OUR LADY OF LOURDES INTERPARISH SCHOOL

Imagination!

I'm being eaten by imagination
It starts in my toes
Wiggles up my legs
Fills up my body
Flies to my head
Then explodes into my brain
Where it eats my thoughts
Burns my skull
Tells me everything

Then it seeps down my arm
And into my fingers

Now out my pen
Onto my paper
It draws a picture and dances 'round
Glides across the blue line

It writes a story

A story for you and me

Michael T. Miller
CHRISTIAN OUTREACH SCHOOL

Field Goal!

The kicker
at the
fifty. Wind
blows in his
face He looks
at the goal
posts. Courage
rises within
him. Then he kicks the ball. No one
breathes. It is high... It is long...
It goes in!
The
crowd
cheers
triumphantly!

Amber Draayer
NORTHERN LIGHTS ABC SCHOOL

Click, Clack

It's a rainy day
And I have nothing to do
So, instead of feeling blue
I'm going to put on my tap shoes.

When the rain falls
It sounds like a drumbeat,
Which makes me want to move my feet.

The toe goes click,
The heel goes clack,
Well, don't you like the sound of that?

Click, click, clack,
I get my cane and hat.
And spin around on my shoes that tap.

The raindrops stop pouring
One by one,
But I don't notice
Because I am having too much fun!
Clack, click, click, clack!

Matteo Giovani Sullivan
ST. ANN CATHOLIC SCHOOL

Skiing through the Woods

Click! My ski boot clicks into my ski binding.
I grab my poles and I'm off. I see the snow glisten.
My papa glides ahead. I breathe out the air while pumping my arms.
I hear the wind pick up. Ski tracks lead me into the woods.
Deer trails are next to the ski trails. The cold bites my face.
Skiing is like life—you never know where the trail will lead you,
back at home or lost in the woods.

Sarah Rose
IMMACULATE CONCEPTION SCHOOL-COLUMBIA

To Be Special… Every Single Time

In the winter layers of frost and ice glint in the soft light
like sheets of glitter dust everywhere.
The frozen gray clouds above blanket all life.
Trees go dormant and animals do too.
Everything sits, so still, so quiet, except for the wind,
the sweet whisper of a lullaby.
This is the season of slumber and rest.

In the spring, the world is made new.
Birds peep merrily in the emerald trees.
Lilacs climb the bushes, filling the air with the light scent of rejuvenation.
Buds burst forth from the once-dead leaves.
This is the season of beginnings.

In the summer, the sun sits high in the sky
like a seemingly unending flash of brilliant luminescence.
Movement is found wherever you look,
in the air, on the ground, or the gently rolling rivers.
Heat radiates through the sunflowers, standing tall with confident might.
Nature is at its peak.
This is the season of dreams come true.

In the fall, leaves put on their daring suit.
Scarlet, daffodil yellow and earthen shades fill the landscape,
setting the land on fire.
Birds come and go in brutal storms, blotting the air like spilled ink.
This is the season of a bold good-bye.

The circle of seasons goes on every year.
Though the pattern repeats itself time and time again,
we find each one to be special…every single time.

Annabelle Brown
MILLSTADT CONSOLIDATED SCHOOL

Christmas Eve

Everyone is gathered around the tree,
With sparkling faces that are full of glee.
They stare up at the twinkling lights,
And admire all the joyful sights.
They gaze at the presents that they all adore,
Until they hear a knock on the door.
They spring to their feet,
To look and see
Who in the world it could be.
Has St. Nicholas come early?
No, it's just Grandma and Grandpa with their presents stacked in a mound.
They widen their eyes as they look all around.
They place their gifts down by the tree,
As the children jump up merrily.
When all is quiet,
And things are settled down,
I tiptoe to the door, not making a sound.
I step outside to enjoy the sights,
Of the glistening, gleaming, glorious lights.
My eyes fall upon a blanket of snow,
And my feet crunch on the earth below.
The lamp on my street is warm and bright,
On this cold, wet, winter night.
I walk into the woods down by the stream,
While the moon gives off a bright white gleam.
And a gust of wind stings my cheek,
As I gaze at the stream which is icy and sleek.
I come back inside to my family,
Talking and singing joyously.
I sit by the fire to warm by the heat,
And I realize that these are the moments that can't be beat.

Helen Baraki
ST. FRANCES CABRINI ACADEMY

The Sunset

The sun setting low
Lighting up the night so bright
It is beautiful

Susan Gibbs
GRAND CENTER ARTS ACADEMY

The Fading Lights

As each minute passed
The light was fading
She held his old hand
And kept him gazing

She held his hand
As he said goodbye
To all of his family
With the light in his eyes

His eyes finally shut
The lights burnt away
And after a while
The monitor didn't sway

It took some weeks after
To fill in the hole
In all of their hearts
And it was a great toll

It's hard to imagine
When you're in her place
But life does go on
At a steady pace

Someday we all
Will be the man in the bed
So be like him then
And love life before death

Edrance Emmanuel
ST. LOUIS PREMIER CHARTER SCHOOL

Can't Stop Me

I sing all day.
People say I can't sing,

That doesn't stop me.

People always say, "No way,
You can't do it."

That doesn't stop me.

People always try to walk over me,
Call me names, say bad things.

Sometimes I think I should end it all
Like a tree ready to fall.

But then I go by my motto:
You can step on me
But you can't stop me.

I'm like the wind.
I might stop,
But I'll come again.

Before people talk about me,
They should know
What I've been through.

People say, "I'm better than you."

I like the motto that I use:
You can step on me
You can even break me

But you can't stop me.

Laillah Al-sahlani
LYON AT BLOW MIDDLE SCHOOL

Light and Dark

The light, forever bright.

When I saw the light kill the dark night,
"Darker and darker!" it shouted...
The light was stronger, no doubt about it.

The rays of the sun shot like a machine gun.
Darkness began to bleed.
The sun was still confident indeed.

Away it fled,
The darkness sped,
The sun's victory made history.

DeAsia Quarrels
DE LA SALLE MIDDLE SCHOOL AT ST. MATTHEW'S

Voiceless

You don't see her shadow.
You don't feel her pain.
She can't see the sun.
All she can see is the rain.

She wants to scream
And wants to be free,
But to her that is just another dream.
She is invisible to everyone else.

The only word she knows is "mean".
She can't speak.
On others she is afraid to lean.

She doesn't love, nor does she trust.
Her heart is full
Of fear's thrust.

She wants to grow. She wants to bloom,
But she stays quiet, fearing the world,
From the back of the classroom.

Never judge a book by its cover, because you don't know the pages that have been torn out.

Tylea Wilson
LIFT FOR LIFE ACADEMY

A Girl's Story

She is always sad like the bullet of a gun
Her family around is always on the run
The music in her room screams her feeling
All her parents are—are hustlers on the street dealing
Tanisha, the depressed intolerant child,
Always has this fierce attitude like an animal in the wild
PA POW is the sound her gun does
A girl aiming at the wrong people is all she ever was
Somebody she begs just to end her life
Before she does it herself with a gun or a knife
This isn't my life, or my life story,
But I pray for this girl that she finds glory

Anthony Jackson
BERKSHIRE JUNIOR-SENIOR HIGH SCHOOL

My Name is Anthony Jackson

Like everybody says roses are red and violets are blue
But in my life it does not come true
Nobody can see what I'm going through
But they do try to see what I go through
And the only things that are red are my rosary beads too

These gangs got me caught up in the moment
But the only thing I can do is get through
And nowadays these kids they are not fighting
Now they are just handling things with 45s, 38s and 22s

People say that heaven is up and hell is down
But it seems like we are in hell
So I have to grind to the fullest

Look over your back everywhere you go

Ethan Bialy
MILLBROOK MIDDLE SCHOOL

The Predator

Perched in the high branches of a tree,
A predator waits for prey.
Glancing around, here and there,
Something good comes his way

Climbing down from his treetop perch,
The hungry anole looks for his lunch.
He walks a short way and comes to a stop.
He's found the prey he wants to munch.

Skillfully stalking his way through the reeds,
A small cricket comes into sight.
With great position and perfect timing,
He chomps down with all of his might!

Perched high in a tree,
A predator wonders who his next victim will be.

Emma Watson
HOLY INFANT SCHOOL

Bystander

I gaze at them
at the city being bombarded
at the buildings crashing down.
Amazement runs through me—
what a couple of words can do
to hurt someone,
to kill someone.

The murderer
and the others laugh
while the victim sits there
with such a pale
blank face,
so blank
it looks like a white piece of paper.

I gaze at them
while the bullies
kill their victim.
I gaze at them
knowing that I'm
a bystander…
but I'm no longer innocent.

Ryshaad Beuford
COMPTON-DREW ILC MIDDLE SCHOOL

My Life

Coming into the world brought my parents joy
I was full of joy
One day that joy turned to pain
On that cold winter day
The car began to slide
Suddenly Bang! Crash! Sigh!
My mother just died
My Uncle didn't see us pulling out of the drive
He didn't stop fast enough so my mother could dive
Dive out of the way to avoid being hit
We were rushed to the hospital
I was permanently injured and suffered pain
Yet, I continue to remember mother's name.
"Tiffany" is what I cry out when I am struggling
She continues to give me strength when I'm weak
Her memory helps me continue to reach
Higher goals in school and out
With my mom by my side
I will never doubt.

Alex Rush
MORRIS FORD MIDDLE SCHOOL

Motivation

Motivation doesn't come naturally
It requires being bold
It's fueled by the things that have been done for me
To get me through the cold

It's like stepping out into the bitter land
A place that is hostile and hopeless
But somehow you reach the warm sands
You feel like you've achieved something and want to be noticed

Although things may stand in your way
Like threats, sadness, anger, or despair
Deep inside there's a ray of sunlight from a summer's day
That creates a fire that starts to flare

You begin to want to fight for what's right
You feel like you could inspire a nation
You could do this for infinite days and infinite nights
This, my friend, is the feeling of motivation

Jamison Jenkins
MARIAN MIDDLE SCHOOL

The Little Red Flame

Fire,
The one thing I truly admire

The way it dies down and comes back to life,
How it can light a room bright … so bright

Orange. Yellow. Red. White
Burning and burning throughout the night

The only thing to keep me warm,
To bring me peace during a storm

So mischievous, you will never see
How it changes course spontaneously

How it dances around in the pit
So entertaining all you can do is sit

Sit and watch the joy it brings
How it makes you want to laugh and sing

Not even sadness can put it to shame,
Because underneath … is a little red flame

Michael Eddleman
LONG MIDDLE SCHOOL

The Spark

As I walk on the sidewalk
And I reach that small park
My brain started drifting
And I felt a small spark
I gazed and I drifted till I swallowed my tongue
I was so restless so stupid and blatantly dumb
To have not of seen what I could have become

So smart I was to not do as I was told
To forget all of this and go run back home
To let go of my dreams
and go home in a dome
Unable to get out all trapped and alone
But I will find this flame
And ignite this small spark
Then I'll fight off this darkness and light up this park

20 Years later I remember that park
And that flame that ignited this spark
and created all of light
So I made this world happy
And lit up the dark
Until one day the darkness was too much for this spark
So I leave this flame for whoever is next
To take on the darkness and finish my quest

Bri Buscher
SUNRISE ELEMENTARY SCHOOL

Running Shoes

Black as night.
Light as day.
Why are you always running away…
From me?
What did I do?
Was it something I said?
What did I do?
Why won't you stay?
I guess you're running away…
in those running shoes again.
I hate Nike,
almost as much as I do you right now.
But, I hate you more
for buying those stupid running shoes.

Peyton Logan
LAKE MARY PREPARATORY SCHOOL

You Are So Annoying

You walk by like you own the place,
When really you do not.
Like you own everything,
When annoying is all you got.

Everything about you screams annoying
Your voice makes my ears bleed.
Attempts of befriending
Psh! between the lines you must read.

You're as kind as Darth Vader combined with Voldemort,
But when what you think comes out of your mouth
I just flat out snort.

You are so annoying.
Every single day.
Yes, you are so annoying.
In every single way.

Someday you'll make me crack
With your irritating ways
You'll make me go wack,
So I'll walk up to you and say,

You are so annoying.
Every single day.
Yes, you are so annoying,
In every single way.

Leave me alone
Before I scream.
Your annoyingness has shown,
To make my unhappy side gleam.

You're not as great as you think you are.
Yes, someday you'll see,
That one person dislikes you,
And that person is me.

Alexandria Noelle Irwin
ST. MARK'S LUTHERAN SCHOOL

The Window

She looks out the window.
Her reflection staring back.
Tears run down her face.
Rain drips down the glass.

Through the window she finds the truth,
Like a rainbow after a storm of lies.
The falsities drip down the glass like the raindrops,
Trickling out of sight.

She wipes away the fog on the pane,
A circle of clarity.
One eye peeks through,
Sees all that she has missed.

Through the fog of lies that have covered the window,
Now she sees, now she knows,
What the truth has shown.

Jennifer Lee
FERN BACON MIDDLE SCHOOL

Angel in Disguise

Even after you neglected us
And forgot our special occasions
Why do I still make a fuss
When we don't celebrate your big day

Mom told you to behave
But temptation was what you craved
So, thoughtlessly, you left us
And returned with a bad reputation

I am confused as to why we still let you in

Actually, why do I still let you in
When I was there to witness your sins
Like a lion, my heart raged with roars
But you tamed my voice
Therefore, my life caves in silence
For I am afraid to say something wrong

So, hopefully, one day
God will find a way
For you to embark on something GOOD!

Because my mom, who loved you more
Became nothing to you but a sore
Yet the ladies who didn't care
You mistook for something too rare

But now I realize it all
Mom said I'm an…
angel in disguise

I'm always ready to catch her when she falls
And when I look in your eyes
I see them full of envy and despise
I guess you shouldn't have messed with

An "angel in disguise"

Angeline Lindsey
GATEWAY MICHAEL SCHOOL

Angel

Angel
Loving, helpful, unique, stubborn
Younger sister of much loved brother nicknamed "Buddy"
Lover of pets especially dogs
Who feels alone in the dark
Who needs everyone's attention
Who gives her love and help to her classmates
Whose eyes light up when she sees a St. Louis Cardinal win
Lives in the "Gateway to the West"
Lindsey

Katya Giffenig
SALISBURY CENTRAL SCHOOL

Sisters

They call me annoying even when it's not true.
They say I'm peculiar but what can I do?
When I ask too many questions they say, "Go away."
When I say, "Let's Play"
They say, "Not today."
If I play with their hair they say I'm too touchy
If I make a concoction
They say, "That's just yucky."

But having two sisters isn't so bad.
They braid my hair and cheer me up when I'm sad.
They pick me up when I fall down.
They make up songs just to fool around.
They'll even be seen in public with me if I promise to calm down.
We may kick, scream, and punch,
But that's only because we love each other a bunch.
So, as you can see, being the youngest of three
May not be as bad as you thought it would be.

Devonte Courtney
PEABODY eMINTS ACADEMY

Boxing

Beat up on each other to see who wins.

Only the undefeated champ for me.

Xtra weight lifting to get stronger.

Improving my skills always.

Never giving up.

Getting punched hard in the body.

Harris Causevic
OUR LADY OF SORROWS CATHOLIC SCHOOL

Beast From The East

Kobe Bryant takes the 3-point shot,
and his opponent knows he doesn't miss a lot.

Born in a wasteland of a town,
he always dreamed of having a golden crown.

He grew up watching the best of the best,
like Magic Johnson who played for the West.

Now that dream has become real,
all his childhood haters realize he's the real deal.

His dad was his biggest inspiration,
now he can send him on vacation.

He is from Pennsylvania in the East,
even Michael Jordan can agree that he is a beast.

People say he doesn't pass the ball,
he can even steal when the opponents are trying to stall.

He's not a point guard,
but in the paint he goes hard.

His classic shot called the fadeaway,
he gets better at it every day.

He got into a brawl with Vince Carter,
before he was close to being a starter.

After the battle, no one can call him a coward,
and the same thing with his fighting teammate Dwight Howard.

He also got another teammate, Steve Nash,
whenever Steve shoots a 3-pointer he makes it splash.

In Los Angles he plays for the Lakers and makes big bucks,
he is fancy and elegant when he wears his new tux.

Now that he is older he is not as fast as a raccoon being chased by a dog,
since he's not as fast as he used to be, you'll sometimes see him jog.

I know that sooner or later that day will come,
and when it does I will be very glum.

I adored him when he was in beast mode,
When he retires my heart will explode.

Elisabeth-Rose Rademacher
ST. MARY'S CATHOLIC SCHOOL

Lingering

Hanging by a thread
Waiting for each small
strand to break

You never thought
it would come to this

The moment you
need to choose

Between a bitter
lesser pain

Or a sweeter
lasting pain

They both hurt
It's your decision
I think you should
fall

They think you should
hang on
We all know who
you are though

Someone indecisive

Someone clueless as
to who you are

Someone who can hang
or fall
Or linger in your
own way

However you choose

Goodbye to
My lingering memory

Matthew Wilson
OUR LADY CATHOLIC SCHOOL

Matthew's Journey

I'm from
purple, ribbons to strides.
From the fake smiles that are hidden tears.
I am from the strong man, the cancer fighter,
whose last breathes I remember as if they were an hour ago.
I am from PanCAN and Siteman,
from doctors and nurses.
I am from the Old Mines wise,
and the Hillsboro crazies.
From the "Be Happy" and the "It's ok to cry's."
I'm from the "he's still with you,"
to "he's with Uncle Tim now,"
and with tears rolling down my face, I wipe them off once more.
I'm from Catherine and Jerry,
from beans and ham with cornbread.
From the legs my grandpa lost to Osteoporosis,
from the leap my dad took to find peace.
On my dresser you will find worn out pictures,
forgotten faces that slipped from my grasp.
I am from those memories,
That brought me to this point.
From the apple that fell under the next tree.

Abbie Meyer
GREEN PARK LUTHERAN SCHOOL

Where I'm From

I am from ponytails
From Nike and Asics
I am from warmth and smiles
All lovely and comforting
Smelling of clean laundry and food cooking
I am from the trees
The roses and the leaves
Smelling fresh, crisp, and sweet
I'm from the Christmas cookies
And strawberry blonde hair
From Mom and from Dad
And Grandpa and Grandma
I'm from the TV watchers and radio listeners.

From listening and saying please and thank you
I am from the Christians
Who serve and obey
I am from St. Louis and Germany
Brats and beer
From the singing of the hymns and the praising of the Lord
I am from a family of caring, following the ones before me.

From the blues and tans in the kitchen
And the pinks and greens of my sheets
From the piles of clothes and the many, many messes
I am from the singers and dancers,
The smiles and tears, the hellos and goodbyes.
I am from kindness.
I am from care.
I am from love.

Helen Ann Stone
IMMACULATE CONCEPTION SCHOOL-DARDENNE

Christmas

Hanging out with friends in the school cafeteria,
We waited with calm but anxious and excited hearts
For the upcoming two week break.
The very next day, the fun began when I was reunited with an old friend.
With excited and cheerful spirits,
We skated and swam at the Rec Plex.

Monday quickly came around the corner.
It was the night of my dance recital.
Practicing on the stage created some distressed, embarrassed,
and frustrated emotions.
This was because it was not the greatest routine,
And my favorite teacher was going to be sitting in the audience.

Luckily my hope for Christmas lightened my spirit.
Feelings of jubilance, love, and passion filled the air.
While enjoying the smiling faces of my family,
We opened presents and
Attended Christmas Mass.

The joy didn't end there.
Welcoming, loving, and cheerful relatives
Greeted me at the door for the Christmas celebration.
Just seeing the three college student cousins
Made me happy inside.

I knew the break was eventually going to end.
To the school's surprise
Came two extra snow days!
The Wednesday back was tense and uneasy
As we tried to get into our school routine.
But when I put that aside,
It was great being back with my friends.

Marissa Menendez
VILLA DUCHESNE

The Stress of Homework

Too much homework to do
in the little amount of time I have.
Just when I believe I have completed the last worksheet,
I find another at the bottom of the pile!

It is ten o'clock and here I sit.
I'm surprised this computer hasn't quit!
I want this poem to be perfect,
but tired eyes just want to shut!

Homework never seems to end,
because my teachers are convinced
that homework…
            is my best friend!

Robert Bordeaux
ST. LOUIS PRIORY SCHOOL

Porter

I got a Christmas puppy,
At least that's what they said,
But when I got him home,
I began to scratch my head.

He looked just like a dog,
'til I saw what he could do,
He jumped from chair to chair
Like a lemur in the zoo.

He climbed up in my face
Just like a tabby cat,
And when I gave him his first bath,
He seemed more like a rat.

I thought he was part sheep,
As I brushed his wooly coat,
But then he kept on climbing high,
Just like a mountain goat.

He then went through our trash,
Like raccoons often do,
Then began the stealing,
He chewed up my new shoe!

Now that I have owned this thing
For darn near two whole years,
I still can't figure out,
Where he got his rabbit ears.

Today when asked what pet I have
I don't know what to say.
At least I won't be guessing
If I'll love him every day.

Katie Alves
NORTHWESTERN REGIONAL MIDDLE SCHOOL

The Dogwood Tree

I look out my window in the morning
to see the little white blossoms
swaying on your tree.
The gentle limbs guard you
and your sleeping soul.
Every time I see that tree dancing in the breeze,
I know you're safe in heaven
watching over me.
I know you stand above us,
but I can't wait until we meet,
my sweet, darling Snowshoe.
You sleep in peace beneath the earth,
yet you soar free above us all.
Your body shall forever rest
in the shelter of your
dogwood tree.

Caroline Laird
ST. JAMES THE GREATER SCHOOL

Calming Words

Talking over breakfast with eggs and hot tea
Playing games—*Life, Kings on the Corner*
Offering Kleenex for my bloodied nose
Adjusting my aggravating tassel at kindergarten graduation
Calming Words

Wanting to exercise too much
Ending up in the ER with a broken arm
Bearing the threatening diagnosis
Changing priorities; preparing for your body`s rebellious fight
Calming words

Traveling to distant places
Planning one-on-one outings
Giving up your fulfilling career
Living the motto YOLO to the fullest; no regrets—going for it
Calming Words

Regret now the rules I`d broken
Miss our conversations each day
Overjoyed I look more like you
Reside in my heart for the rest of my life—my Guardian Angel
Calming Words

Bridget Dawson
LITTLE FLOWER CATHOLIC SCHOOL

Ripples

Drop a stone into the water
In a moment it is gone
But there are a hundred ripples
Circling on and on and on.
Say an unkind word this moment
In a moment it is gone
But there are a hundred ripples
Circling on and on and on
Say a word of joy and splendor
In a moment it is gone
But there are a hundred ripples
Circling on and on and on

Chloe Higgins
ST. PAUL CATHOLIC SCHOOL

Thank You

Thank You, Lord, for everything You do.
I love everything out and through, just because it was made by You.
For the trees that give me cool shade,
And the beautiful sight in fall when the leaves' colors fade.
For the light blue sky,
And all the beautiful butterflies and birds that fly,
For the stars so bright that light the dark and gloomy night.
For the sunrise so amazing every day; I hope it never goes away.
For the deep blue oceans full of tiny fish,
And the valleys, mountains, and plains which I cherish.
For my family and every friend,
And our brave soldiers, who protect and defend.
For all the creatures on this world in which we live,
And for a good life, which to me You give.
Thank You, Lord, for this strong and amazing nation.
Thank You, Lord, for all of creation.

Shon Nelson
GATEWAY MIDDLE SCHOOL

My Mom

My mom is black, beautiful, and strong.
She excels and is determined to survive
In a world that can be brutal.
She is unfazed by obstacles that try to block her way.
She looks back through time
And realizes she must maintain
Her strong will of invincibility to succeed
Regardless of her past.
My mom is black, bold, and beautiful,
And the most important piece of the puzzle,
We call her Mother Earth!

Michael Drabelle
ACADEMY OF THE SACRED HEART

The Beauty of the Night

The beauty of the night is what man might not see—
But to one who looks closely, it portrays royalty.
Throughout the Earth, in abstract ways,
Though subtle, though hidden, its wonder it conveys:
With a scattered sounding forest or an open plain
And the cry of the wolf to let out inner pain,
Through the nocturnal creatures which we only hear
Or those great bright eyes that make all appear.

Furthermore, the dark sky can be misunderstood,
For the moon and the stars do what the sun never could:
Fitting light with darkness gives gorgeous glamour,
Filling a night's image without any failure.
So quite clear, it is such a beautiful sight—
Unnoticed, but we should see, the beauty of the night.

John Calio
REGINA COELI SCHOOL

The Midnight Hunter

Through the darkened skies of night,
flies the winged owl, keen and bright.
Sitting in the moonlit branches,
that are the owl's banquet hall,
or on the roofs of silent ranches,
overseeing the deeds of all.

Hoo! His call, sorrowful and repetitive,
acts like a heavy sedative.
A special bird is the owl,
not just a simple little fowl.
The owl is a wise creature,
wisdom, an excellent feature.

Jemma Aline Moccasin
KLEIN ELEMENTARY SCHOOL

Life

What is life?

Most people never realize how precious life is
Until their life is almost gone.
I've heard elders tell me regrets they have had in their lives.
I have many regrets just like the others.

After I had lost my father, I realized how precious one's life is.
He did lots to help other people, and he loved what he did.
He made the most out of his life for he knew he didn't have long.
He told me his reason for living was because he knew I was coming.

I hope to make my father proud.
I wish more people could be like him.
I wish people would love who they are
And what they do.

What is life?

Instead of hearing people say they love their life,
I hear them say they hate their life and themselves.
I know someone like this. She is a good person,
But she feels bullied and… for what reason?

She doesn't understand, so she doesn't talk anymore.
She isn't who she used to be; she's afraid to make a mistake.
I miss her; I miss who she used to be.
Why do people hurt others? Is it because they have been hurt themselves?

What is life?

Hurting others is not okay. When you see someone hurting others,
Have you ever thought why? Has he or she been hurt too?
Is that the cause of most bullying?
Everyone targets the bully, calling them bad.

At times I feel sorry for the bully.
I wonder what has happened to make him or her that way.
I hope one day the hurting goes away;
No pain, no fights, no violence.

What is life?

I want people to get along, and disagreements can be healthy.
Fights that turn to violence are not okay.
Not everyone has to like each other; not everyone has to be friends,
But we need to stand among one another and stick up for each other.

So...if you see someone being hurt
Then do something.
Anything would be helpful
To a person in need.

What is life?

Will this question ever be answered? I guess it doesn't matter.
All that matters is that you learn to love yourself.
Learn to love your life; learn to love your mistakes.
Mistakes are healthy; learn from those mistakes.

What is life?
Life is temporary,
Death is not.
What is life?

Haley Pate
JEFFERSON MIDDLE SCHOOL

My Bully

Please tell me where things went wrong
We were friends, best as can be
So, what happened?
Please tell me
Just give me a reason!
Is there a problem?
It's eating at me -"What did I do??!!"
I hear you laughing
I know it's at me
I see you point
I see you stare
I hear you laughing
My "bestie"
My bully

Grace Schwartz
ST. ROCH SCHOOL

You Will Never Know

They think she isn't sorry
for the things in the past she's done.
Or that she doesn't care
about the damage that has come.
But she hurts, she cries, and hides it
under a carefree grin
While inside a child is crying from within.
I am this girl I speak of
and it hurts me to say,
what has happened to me since my birth
and to this current day.
You've seen it in the movies
or on the TV screen.
But what you've witnessed from your seats
are real experiences to me.
They hurt, they hit, they scowl,
and fail to realize
that though the marks do fade,
the pain remains,
and I am left a broken child.
Sometimes I wake up crying,
or go to bed afraid,
But my horror follows me morning 'til night,
and all through my days.
Now you know my story,
and how my life does go.
Still, you say you understand,
but you will never know.

Eden Spiva
BUSCH MIDDLE SCHOOL OF CHARACTER

Why Do I Want To?

You hurt me, you truly did.
    Why are you in my mind?
        I'm so confused.
How could you come out against me?
    You've turned my world upside down.
        Yet I still stand.
Why are you in my mind?

That is the question.
    Do I believe what they say?
        That you are popular?
That I want to be you?
    Should I turn like the rest?
        No, no, no. I shall stay who I am no matter what.
Everyone wants to belong.

I have not yet reached the breaking point.
    There are just so many questions that I must ask.
        Why, no matter what I do ... Do you ignore me?
Everyone wants to belong.

Why? Why does everyone want to belong?
    Are we just trying to be remembered, even accepted?
        "Live" while we're young?
Or is it just because nobody wants to be ignored?

You act as if I am not here.
    Is it just because I am speaking the truth?
        Trust me this is no threat, but just think for a moment.
Everyone wants to belong,
    and no one can take that freedom away.
        The freedom to wish, I am a soldier and always will be.

That's why I want to.

Ruben Oseguera
STEVENS CENTER FOR ACADEMIC DEVELOPMENT

Respect

Worrying about respect is what got me into trouble in the first place.
You see . . . grown people need respect from kids.
Kids need respect from grownups.
What other respect is there?
Well, football players . . . respect each other.
Basketball players . . . respect each other?
Out of respect they battle each other for a championship.
But you can't spend your whole life fighting for respect.
It's a win-lose situation.
People will disrespect you for no reason.
Disrespect is one of the main reasons why people fight!
Don't let anyone steal your joy!
People are not in control of all your happiness.
Does respect thrill your soul?
Why do you need so much respect?
Now think about it . . . what is the problem with respect?
Or, is Respect the real problem?
Maybe people are the real problem.
They go around blaming everybody.
They even blame the world.
They are never at fault.
When you are angry with one particular person,
You have to remember that you are not angry with the world.
And don't say you were really mad, because only dogs go mad.
Are you big enough?
Does it really matter who's to blame?
Why don't you suck it up?
After all what's the big deal?
Don't lose any sleep over it because life still goes on!
You have to always remain strong.

Chloe Fletcher
ANTONIA MIDDLE SCHOOL

This Little Song Called Darling

There's this little song called *Darling*
That brings back lots of thoughts
For every time I hear this song
It haunts and haunts and haunts

This song brings back bad memories
That I've tried to just let go
This is why we all have secrets
For we can't let our sorrow show

This little song called Darling
Always brings me to tears
For when I hear the lyrics
I just want to shut my ears

Self-harm, Anorexia
All these things bring back great pain
These things can tear someone apart
And leave them deep in pain

I can see the hate in people's eyes
I can sense the sadness
I can tell if you want to stop and cry
Because I have dealt with this madness

You look in the mirror
And don't like what you see
So you turn around and walk away
Just leave the reflection be

You don't have a thigh-gap
You don't have a perfect figure
You don't have a flat stomach
And you couldn't possibly be bigger

These things I just described
Can poison one's mind
This thing is called Anorexia
And it is never kind

You wear bracelets almost every day
That go all the way up your arm
You say it's only fashion
But I know it's self-harm

Every night after school
You go home and cry
Your dad doesn't like you
You can see it in his eyes

Your mom is always insulting you
And putting you down
She tells you you're not good enough
So you always wear a frown

All these thoughts spin through your head
You don't know what else to do
So you slide your blade against your wrist
Then down go your sleeves; no one has a clue

All these things I just described
Can drive someone insane
Especially when the thoughts won't leave
And they're stuck inside your brain

Someone out there cares about you
Don't let them tell you otherwise
You may think it's silly
But you're an angel in disguise

This little song called *Darling*
Is about all of these things
So please stop hating yourself
It's not time to grow your wings

Dillon Walter
BERKSHIRE CHRISTIAN SCHOOL

Stop

Hello red stop
sign with your letters in
white. You guide me while
turning to the left and to the right.
At night you shine with your shimmering
glow, so we understand when to stop and
go. Your octagonal shape is pleasing to the
eye. You protect me so I don't crash
and die. Thank you for keeping
me safe and sound. I'm sure
I'll see you next
time around.

Josephine Harris
CENTRAL JUNIOR HIGH SCHOOL

Hiding in the Trees

I see you
down there
hiding in the trees
away from all troubles
safe as can be.

As soon as you come out
you're surrounded by hate
you try to run away
trying to escape.

You are the creator
of this living place
it is no one else's
but your mistake.

While you're running away
you think to yourself
what have I done
how can I remake.

There's no way to fix this
it is permanent now
stuck in your head
a lesson learned for your own sake.

You must face this now
do not be afraid
be strong, be fearless
and don't run away.

Haley Oetterer
ST. VINCENT DE PAUL SCHOOL

Believing, The Hardest Thing To Do...

Believing, the hardest thing to do...
Deep down in my heart, in my soul, in my mind and body,
I know it is not real,
But I choose to believe.
All those books that I read,
Those fairy tales, enchanted castles, brave heroes,
great adventures, dangerous beasts, and wonders of all kinds.
I know they aren't real, but I choose to believe,
Even though I see with my eyes, smell with my nose,
taste with my tongue, hear with my ears, and feel with my skin.
Deep down I know they aren't real, but on the crust of my skin
I still wish and believe they are real. I always will believe.
It's blended in my heart all the way to my soul.
I choose to believe.

Andrew Tague
ST. JOAN OF ARC CATHOLIC SCHOOL

In A World

Be in a world where you can create whatever,
Do whatever,
See whatever.

Be in a world with the deepest of caves,
And with the scariest of monsters.

Be in a world where you can make the strongest armor,
And find the shiniest of ores.

Be in a world where you defeat your friends,
And blow up their creations.

Be in a world where it's made of blocks
And your name is Steve.

Be in a world where you start off punching a tree,
And end in a place with diamonds on your chest.

And this world sounds like a fantasy,
But this world is a fantasy.

A game fantasy.

A game called Minecraft.

Jeffrey Ho
MCKINLEY CLASSICAL LEADERSHIP ACADEMY

The Four Sword

Pull the sword out of its pedestal}
but be warned

The moment you grab its hilt
and point the blade's tip to the heavens

Your soul will be split into four

One fragment for each element

One soul filled with rage and energy,
He shall hold the flames

One soul as sad and as blue as the ocean,
He shall hold the water

One soul, sincere and forgiving,
He shall hold the Earth

And one soul of brave heart and heroic thought,
He shall hold the winds

That soul
Is your soul

Reilly Tucker
ST. MICHAEL SCHOOL OF CLAYTON

Chaos

i wander into the chaos
a chill runs up my spine

they scream and yell and fight
but can't hear me
even though i try with all my might

a tear runs down my face like a raindrop in a storm
the emotions i want to express still do not form

the words i speak evaporate
into the surrounding air

i cannot run i cannot hide
there's nowhere else to look for pride

the ocean in a hurricane
is more calm than all this pain

Jayden Palmer
HILLCREST SCHOOL

Escape

As I try to escape this place
I see all of the people who need me,
But I want to make my own decisions.
I understand how you say I am too young.
But don't you say live life to the fullest,
Or how I should learn from my mistakes?
Maybe I should make more mistakes.

I also see people like me who don't like it here,
And they try to escape through books, movies, and music.
But when the movie ends, the song comes to a speeding halt,
Or when you finish that line,
You are still reminded that
Growing up takes time

Kyra Chanae Conner
HAZELWOOD SOUTHEAST MIDDLE SCHOOL

We've Got To Do Better

We've got to do better in all the things we do.
We've got to do better because someone is watching you.
We've got to do better at doing our very best.
We've got to do better while we're at these desks.
We've got to do better is a phrase adults often say.
But, they have to do better by showing us the way.

Stephen Dewitt
RAPID CITY SDA ELEMENTARY SCHOOL

Lady

This great bird
Bearing down on her target
Gracefully she drops
Plummeting downward
To and from her nest
Wild nesting eagle
Gentle mother hen
Taking part in motherhood
Laying her first egg

Porter Hankins
TRINITY SCHOOL OF MIDLAND

The Fierce Queen

She has the beauty of an angel,
the voice of a queen,
but when you anger her, she is quite mean.
She's always there for me, and I with her,
never will we forever part.

We get into fights about the strangest things,
and she'll always win with her power over me.
My best method is to let her cool down,
and for the fire to come out of her beautiful crown.

She is always in my heart, no matter which way you put it,
and she will always be, forever more,
my beautiful mom.

Will Webster
ST. GABRIEL THE ARCHANGEL SCHOOL

Mia and Me

Her skin is brown,
mine is white.
I love to run,
she loves to bike.

She plays soccer,
I play lacrosse.
I try to tell her what to do,
She thinks she's the boss.

To aggravate her is my goal,
to shriek at me is hers.
I hope she knows this will never change.
What else would she expect from her brother?

God knew she was the one for us,
without Him we'd have missed her.
She came home to us when I was three,
I love my little sister.

Lucy Ward
ST. LOUIS CHRISTIAN ACADEMY

Fluttering Hearts

As we stand on the rocks by the sea,
My feet are ready to flee.

I need to speak from the heart,
But I know not where to start.

As I speak I stutter,
Because my heart is aflutter
For you.

Julianna Nasi
WAPPINGERS JUNIOR HIGH SCHOOL

Ode To My Annoying Siblings

My dear siblings,
With love and care
Fighting like superheroes and villains

We tease and chase each other
Screaming hoarsely,
Waiting for the other to roar.
One of us wins the fight.
Off runs the whiner.
They work it out
With some whines of sorrow.

I can hear my sister singing higher
than the heavens.
She's singing on the edge
Waiting to be discovered
While the other sister is upstairs.
She sets the table for dinner
Clitter
Clatter
Of the plates.
With a holler everyone comes
Everyone, with their elephant stomps.

By nightfall the little brothers
Or should I say little bothers
Settle down
Giving out hugs and kisses,
Waiting to be tucked in their nests
Along with their bedtime story.

They fall asleep
Dreaming of superheroes
Fighting with a pow.
So they smile in their sleep
Of the heroes' great defeat.
At last, our silence has begun.

Alexis Kleekamp
LASALLE SPRINGS MIDDLE SCHOOL

Piano

I place my fingers on the keys and go
Starting out soft and slow
And growing fast and loud
Boom, Boom, Crash

Jumping chords and melodies
Sounding as loud as thunder
All of a sudden I am a mouse

Phrasing dynamics, voicing and rhythm
Crescendo and decrescendo, artistry and more
So much to think about
So much to do

And then like that I'm done
I finished, it was good
But not good enough
I lay my fingers on the keys and go again

Corinna Davidson
ANNIE WRIGHT DAY SCHOOL

Rules of the Mouse

Scurry, nibble, nose twitch, hide.
Those are the instructions I hear inside.

No others know the steady beat
I follow as I move my feet.

Ear perk, climb up, higher than high;
Feels like I could touch the sky.

Smaller than small, faster than lightning,
Still there are those who find me frightening.

Heart pound, dodge paw, stay alive;
Here is my pressure to survive.

Those who die, they are the fools.
Those who live have these same rules.

Scurry, nibble, nose twitch, hide.
By these rules I must abide.

Jessica Stacker
KIPP INSPIRE ACADEMY

Words With No Meaning

The ones nobody seems to understand,
Too abstract.
So we contemplate.

Take it apart,
Put it back together.
Rearrange the letters,
As if we're playing Scrabble.

No such books will help.
No words we couldn't understand anymore.
The day has passed,
The sun has set.

Nobody to teach us.
No leaders.
But we don't cry,
Even when it's out of our reach.

We still keep thinking.
No one seems to know.
But we ask ourselves,
Do all words have meaning?

Joey Dougherty
ST. CATHERINE LABOURE SCHOOL

The Pen

I am a pen,
Leaping for the blank white page
Eager to write and draw inspiring tales
Tracing lines up and down the paper
Feeling the motions of the desktop below me

Drawing creativity with ink,
I place black upon white like a chessboard.
I like to write stories with my swift motions.
I feel energy rush through me when I create worlds with my mind.

Unlike a pencil, I am not messy.
The pencil lines smudge at random.
But I am the swift and sturdy pen.
I create stories in the blink of an eye.

Ink staining, I race up the page.
Lines sketching back and forth,
I create ideas on paper.
I am the mighty pen.

The pen saved lives.
The pen crossed seas.
The pen stops hunger.

How?
Humans use the pen.
They sketch laws and rules.
They write letters and essays.

The pen inspires.
I inspire.
I am the pen.

Rose Steinhart
ST. CLARE OF ASSISI SCHOOL

Perfect

Perfect is a word that cannot describe me
Because I, like everyone else, have flaws you can or cannot see
I may not be the prettiest or the smartest in the grade
But I am who I am, because this is how I was made
We think perfect is a word that means beautiful, smart, and kind
But to me, flawless isn't the word that comes to mind
Perfect means to embrace your flaws and be proud
I, for one, can be a bit annoying and loud
I don't have the best clothes or the prettiest hair
And if I'm being honest sometimes I do care
But instead of complaining I stick a smile on my face
Because those flaws are what have made me different in the first place
Maybe if we all could just be ourselves we could see how great it can feel
To show people who we really are instead of hiding ourselves to be
Concealed.

Rylie Bunning
ST. JOSEPH SCHOOL

Trapped

I listen to the wind whistle through the screen.
Rain batters the house.
I hear thunder rumble in the distance.
Lightning flashes to the ground.

I turn from the window jealous.
How free the clouds are to come and go as they please!
How I wish I could do the same,
but alas, I am trapped in the way of this life.

Trapped by the judges.
They judge you if you are different.
They judge if you stray from the beaten path.
They judge if you don't want to be like everyone else.

Oh! How technology has trapped us within ourselves!
No technology? No social life.
No text messages? No friends.
We are trapped by each other.

We are trapped by ourselves.

K'Hayla Z. Smith
CONFLUENCE ACADEMY-SOUTH CITY

You

Stop running away from yourself.
You act like being yourself is such a crime.
You just sit there while your feelings are eating you alive.
Just let it all out, and tell the world you've had enough.
Then maybe life won't seem so tough!
Critics may break or beat you down, but all you have to say is…
I'm ready to be me now.

Sherron Ivory
LOYOLA ACADEMY OF ST. LOUIS

Do You Matter

You are fast
You are slow
Does it matter
No it don't
But do you matter
Maybe you do
I don't know
How about you

Do you want to be a clown
Then turn that frown upside down
I look at you with respect
You look at me from neck to neck
But do it matter

You can do the wrong, good, even bad
But you're not making me mad
You can do any occasion
It don't matter if you're hispanic or caucasian
It don't matter but you do matter
You're just putting your soul all over the platter

It's your choice just make it matter
You can be like dwyane wade
Just do it right and make the fade
But do you matter

If you can see what I can see
I'll tell you what you mean to me
If you see black and I see white
But do it matter
I guess it might

You're getting closer and closer
You're almost there
Keep on trying you'll get here
Just don't pull out another hair
Do you matter just keep it fair

Slow it down
You are not going to lose
You will win this battle and that's good news
Do you matter
Yes you really do

Tasanya Roberts
PAMOJA PREP ACADEMY

The Dark Piece of Chocolate From the House on the Right

I am a dark chocolate female from the house on the right,
A birthday on the 8th but I'm gonna party tonight
I'm gonna grow up successful and my future's so bright
But watch me be an inspiration and touch that bright light

'Cause…

I work hard, get them As
I don't care about what you say
I get good grades, study everyday
all work getting done, I don't even play
now what you say now
I'm walking
hush up little girl—now I'm talking
I'm tryna teach you something that you could study Sunday
so that you could pass that test on Monday

'Cause…

I am that little girl growing up to be what I want to be
with the brown skin and glasses
you see
I was born at the Forest Park Hospital
Sounds of laughter fill the air
getting chased by that girl with the beautiful brown hair
When I was younger I remember I was that happy little girl in that
purple shirt and those khaki pants running around the playground

Now…

Right here and right now,
I am like a picture in his or her dreams.
Tomorrow I will be a successful young lady and they will want to be like me
That young lady whose name starts with a T and that's me
Tasanya Roberts you see.

Ayanna Elaine McCoy
HIGH MOUNT SCHOOL

Timeless Love

Love is strong and can't be controlled.
Love can last a lifetime if it wanted.
No one can fight love.
Love is not a virus or a sickness.
It runs through our veins like blood.
It's been with us since the dawn of time.
Before the dinosaurs and humans
The only thing is …
Is that we have to make the choice to accept it.

Jordan Morris
SOUTH CITY PREPARATORY ACADEMY

The Golden Sun Vein

Rough and ashamed
Twisting turning with excruciating pain
Heartwarming wipes
Living secrets and scary flight

Breaking away from salvation
You shouldn't get more appreciation
Royal young humming the singing
Spoken to this devilish kingdom
I can't break away for freedom

Blood is rich and thicker than water
You don't want to live in trapping slaughter
It's like trickling acid burning through my veins
Cold crushing ice in the palm of my hand
Living that's your screaming fan

Looking out of the blue sea
Away from the shadowy surface
The red golden blood rushing through my veins
Well that's my living fame

Heart pounding, mind racing, crooked smile
It could get killed easily
More willing to foul
Attitude choices is the number one thing
Dreaming is your bridge that's above everything

Dancing in freedom you really do need 'em
Instead of frozen like a sheet of ice
You're broken like a speck of ice
Friend, family burn and never die

Your value never be shy
Open and imagination, using people's appreciation
Pure and fun
Well, your veins are pure and golden like the sun

Angela Nguyen
SALEM LUTHERAN SCHOOL - AFFTON

Kidnapped By Sin, Rescued By Faith

Trapped in the darkness, nowhere to go.
Demons surround me, each with a sneer.
I run and tremble with fear.
The demon Envy trails behind me,
Greed and Anger beside him.
I don't know where to go or what to do. They come closer and closer.
I feel my legs start to give up. I look to God and start to pray,
hoping He won't let me stay. I look ahead. Not faraway
is a ray of light.
Envy starts to grab my leg
but I stay strong in this fight.
I see God's hand reaching out
and I grasp it, holding
on tight. Once I'm in the light
the demons have lost this fight.
Now I'm here with God, to serve,
to love, to strengthen my faith.

Aakilah McCoy
GRAND PRAIRIE FINE ARTS ACADEMY

The Reality of Fear

The obstacles in life
Are often strife.
You're not afraid of the
Dark,
You're afraid of
What's in it.
You're not afraid of heights,
You're afraid of
Falling.
You're not afraid to
Race,
You're afraid to
Lose.
You're not afraid of
Trying,
You're afraid of
Failing.
You're not afraid of
Performing,
You're afraid of
Being known.
Don't worry you're not
Alone.
The obstacles in life
Are often strife.

William Scruggs
YEATMAN-LIDDELL MIDDLE SCHOOL

My Song

I don't love the life I live.
Heart is lost, no love to give.
Reality broke—nothing is real.
I have no nerves, so I can't feel.
I have no one by my side.
Brain is lost. I have no guide.
I was blind, now I see.
Everything has a purpose...but me.
I bear no bruises or fears.
I shed no blood or tears.
I don't know right from wrong.
I came to tell my story, so here is my song.

Karli Prue
O'KREEK MIDDLE SCHOOL

Anxiety

There is an insane person inside my body.
You could see her in the way my hands shake when I get nervous.
You could hear her in the way I scream when I get angry.
You could feel the way she stares into your soul through my eyes.
These lines are spoken in her voice, not mine.

Erin Somes
LEE MIDDLE AND HIGH SCHOOL

Nobody Knows…

Nobody knows who I am.
When the doors are closed.
When I am in a room by myself,
I pretend to be someone I want to be.

When I am listening to music,
I see myself on stage
In front of thousands upon thousands of fans.
But nobody knows that.

When I am looking at quotes,
I see those quotes as tattoos.
I see myself covered in tattoos.
But nobody knows that.

I see myself as a lot of things.
A singer/songwriter.
A fighter.
A tattoo artist.
But nobody knows that.

I am someone who overthinks everything.
And I have no idea what to do.
To stop it.
Or what to do about it.

I am afraid to be me because I don't know.
I don't know if people will look or think of me differently.
I don't know if people will like me anymore.
I don't know if they will think that I am crazy.

But that's what I am.
A crazy, antisocial, ratchet, dark person.
That is the person that I am and the person that nobody knows.

Lauren Desmond
HOLY REDEEMER SCHOOL

Only Orphan

I am lost.
It was a big cost.
So no one wants me.
Will I always be lonely?

I was scared.
No one ever cared.
Shy, in a corner,
like a little mourner.

Will I ever be loved?
I am to the side, shoved.
Still searching for my soul
which has a big hole.

Full of pain,
I am going insane.
I am a misfit.
I will never benefit.

Just waiting for a family,
I know it won't appear magically.
Will I ever have an adoption?
Right now, I am just in destruction.

Bethlehem Arrastia-Nowak
WOODSTOCK DAY SCHOOL

I am Like a Caterpillar

Scared like a caterpillar
Slow, young, and unlearned.
Waiting, waiting,
Until I can change
Into something great,
Wise and brave.
For a long time I watch, listen, and learn.
For a long time I tried to live the life I was given,
But something comes to take it away.
Have I not been patient?
Have I not been patient?

On summer's wake,
I changed into something grand.

Karma McKinley
COULTERVILLE JUNIOR HIGH SCHOOL

Summer Petals

As the summer comes, I grow and I grow.
My petals are of beauty.
As it rains, I feel stronger.
I need the sun to shine down longer.

As it warms me, I grow and grow.
My petals are of beauty.
As it rains, I feel strong.
But I feel queasy, and it goes all wrong.

As my neighbors
And I bow our heads,
My petals begin to fall.
Summer's over once again.
My petals are no longer of beauty

We wait and wait.
For summer to come.
Oh, Summer, why are you taking so long?
Beautiful flowers will return.
Even though we wait and wait,
We will live again.

Ian Cordell
ST. JOHN THE BAPTIST ELEMENTARY SCHOOL

Fate

It has no eyes,
yet always sees.
It has no ears,
yet always hears.
It has no heart,
yet is alive.

It knows what has happened,
what is happening,
and what is to come.
Some days it is your enemy,
but other days it is your friend.
It brings you great pain,
but also great joy.

It has brought you here,
reading what I have written.
It has brought me here,
to write what I have written.

Now try to think,
think of what I have said,
of what I could be describing.
You know it,
just let the word flow,
Listen.
It is whispering in your ear.
Then you start to listen
and, like a surge of energy,
you realize I am talking
about
Fate.

Joshua Macy
ALASKA NATIVE CULTURAL CHARTER SCHOOL

Lucky Lake

There was a time when Lucky Lake waited for us to find it
And one day fish there...offering us the fish that swim about

A muskrat visited, almost like it was wishing us luck
The ducks that fly over look at the fish from the sky

Lucky Lake...a place where there is life everywhere...the houses that
Surround it in a circle comfort it like a blanket

And it's always there when we go back
And it will always be there when we go back

When we leave...it will be waiting for us to come back
And fish again

Noelle Hogrebe
ST. RAPHAEL THE ARCHANGEL SCHOOL

The Forest at Night

A silent pond shivers by in the woods,
sparkling it dapples the shore.
A moon hangs in the midnight sky,
an owl begins to soar.

A deer snuffles by some roots,
a mouse scurries away.
The trees all seem to be sleeping,
the leaves dead like decay.

A silent wind whispers through the trees,
the leaves are scattered about.
The crickets play their songs tonight,
the fireflies' lights wink out.

The morning sun is far away,
the darkness is a chilling bite.
Murkiness hangs everywhere,
this is the forest at night.

Grace Stotler
CHRISTIAN FELLOWSHIP SCHOOL

All These Poems

All these poems are floating in my mind.
Some are mean and some are kind.
I must catch them and write them all down.
Some are lost and some are found.

I carry them with me where ever I go.
I carry them with me in the sun and snow.
In the spring and fall, they follow me around,
And even when I can't be found.
I want them here all written down.

So I must write as fast as I can
With great care so people will understand.
For now I will carry on.

But when I must say so long
To those that I hold dear,
"All These Poems" will be right here.

INDEX BY LAST NAME

INDEX BY STATE & SCHOOL

Monroe
Immaculate Conception School-Columbia, *Sarah Rose—66*

Randolph
Coulterville Junior High School, *Karma McKinley—143*

Sangamon
Jefferson Middle School, *Haley Pate—105*

St. Clair
Central Junior High School, *Josephine Harris—88*
High Mount School, *Ayanna Elaine McCoy—134*
Millstadt Consolidated School, *Annabelle Brown—67*

MASSACHUSETTS

Berkshire
Berkshire Christian School, *Dillon Walter—111*
Clarksburg Elementary School, *Aaron Williams—34*
Lee Middle and High School, *Erin Somes—140*

MISSOURI

Boone
Our Lady of Lourdes Interparish School, *Ashley Nicole Hrdina—62*
Christian Fellowship School, *Grace Stotler—147*

Jefferson
Our Lady Catholic School, *Matthew Wilson—91*
Our Lady Queen of Peace School, *Gracie Scanga—58*
Christian Outreach School, *Michael T. Miller—63*
Antonia Middle School, *Chloe Fletcher—109*
Hillsboro R-3 Junior High School, *Mackenzie Goff—46*
Sunrise Elementary School, *Bri Buscher—81*

Lincoln
First Baptist Christian Academy, *Faith Kassebaum—41*

St. Charles
Academy of the Sacred Heart, *Michael Drabelle—101*
All Saints Catholic School, *Danny Behlmann—37*
Immaculate Conception School-Dardenne, *Helen Ann Stone—93*
St. Joseph School, *Rylie Bunning—129*

INDEX BY STATE & SCHOOL

NEW MEXICO

Bernalillo

Native American Community Academy, *Kaleb Palmer—117*

San Miguel

Pecos Middle School, *Alyssa Benavidez—61*

Sandoval

Cochiti Middle School, *Marlene Dominguez—60*

NEW YORK

Columbia

Hawthorne Valley Waldorf School, *Marie Divecchio—26*

Berkshire Junior-Senior High School, *Anthony Jackson—74*

Dutchess

Regina Coeli School, *John Calio—102*

Millbrook Middle School, *Ethan Bialy—75*

Wappingers Junior High School, *Julianna Nasi—123*

Ulster

Woodstock Day School, *Bethlehem Arrastia-Nowak—142*

New Paltz Middle School, *Jordan Mattsen—23*

Rondout Valley Middle School, *Josh Heuvel-Horwitz—44*

SOUTH DAKOTA

Pennington

Rapid City SDA Elementary School, *Stephen Dewitt—119*

North Middle School, *Michael Milk—30*

Todd

Klein Elementary School, *Jemma Aline Moccasin—103*

Littleburg Elementary School, *Tyvon Herman—38*

O'Kreek Middle School, *Karli Prue—139*

Spring Creek Elementary School, *Shelby Little Shield—40*

TEXAS

Bell

St. Mary's Catholic School, *Elisabeth-Rose Rademacher*—*90*

Dallas

Grand Prairie Fine Arts Academy, *Aakilah McCoy*—*137*

Midland

Trinity School of Midland, *Porter Hankins*—*120*
Hillcrest School, *Jayden Palmer*—*117*

WASHINGTON

Pierce

Annie Wright Day School, *Corinna Davidson*—*125*
Morris Ford Middle School, *Alex Rush*—*78*

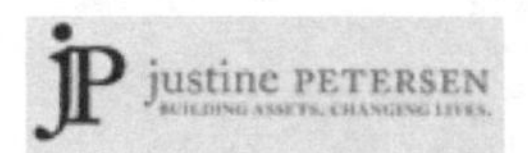

HUSCH
BLACKWELL

ACKNOWLEDGMENTS

This educational literary arts program is only possible because of the courage, dedication and hard work of the educators who gave their students the chance to participate in our open-themed poetry writing contest. We thank each educator for the time and effort they invested to enhance their students' lives, their school, and their community through our program.

This poetry anthology was produced with the generous ongoing financial support of Justine PETERSEN, William A. Kerr Foundation, Regional Arts Commission of St. Louis, Art & Education Council of Greater St. Louis, Missouri Arts Council, and individual contributions by all members of the 7GP Board of Directors. We are also grateful for the year-round support and donations from the Sheraton St. Louis City Center Hotel & Suites.

We are grateful to Husch Blackwell LLP, Anders CPAs & Advisors, and Volunteer Lawyers and Accountants for the Arts for their generous contributions of professional services.

This program year was supported by a team of dedicated staff and supporters. A special thank you to Greg Abler, Cindy Buehler, Jennifer Goldring, Bonnie Kruger, Marisol Ramirez, Robert Boyle, Alexis Turim, Victoria Townson, Mark Wilensky and Freeman Word.

Finally, so much of my passion and vision to improve others' lives is inspired by the spirit and lessons of my parents and their parents. You are all always with me and I thank you.

Aaron Williams
Founder and Champion
The 7th Grade Poetry Foundation

The foundation was conceived and founded by its champion, Aaron Williams. He is Founder and President of Aaron Consulting, Inc., a nationwide attorney search firm based in St. Louis for the past 34 years. Reading and writing poetry combined with a commitment to helping others through innovative approaches have enriched his life. Aaron Williams was a recipient of the 2005 Focus St. Louis "What's Right With the Region" Award for creating and improving educational opportunities in the St. Louis area. He was one of 10 winning poets in the 2013 Poetry in Motion Contest in St. Louis.

Visit www.7GP.org to learn more about The 7th Grade Poetry Foundation.